PRO$PER NOW!

Why wait?

John Wolcott Adams

Published by Golden Key Publications
P. O. Box 30989 Phoenix, AZ 85046-0989 USA

My thanks to **Charlene Rashkow** who so kindly and expertly edited the Pro$per Now Inspirations found in this book. Charlene is an exellent and experienced Writing Stylist, and the author of *Movin' On Up - Business Success on the Internet.* (310) 514-4844
www.allyourwritingneeds.com

ISBN-0-9602166-8-5
Library of Congress Control Number: 2003096366

Printed in the United Stares of America.
10 9 8 7 6 5 4 3 2 1

Books by John Wolcott Adams

Positively Alive!
How To Have 'Unexpected' Income
BE What You Are: LOVE
How I CAN Have Everything!
Thirty Days To A Better Life
Power Words For Prosperous Living
Life is Choice
Pro$per Now!

Dedication

This book is lovingly dedicated to my Master Mind Partner, Barbara Moseley. Thank you, Barbara, for your faithfulness, loving kindness, positive support and helpfulness in so many wonderful ways. You are loved and appreciated.

*Do all you can to fill your mind
with prospering ideas. The more
you charge your mind with
prospering ideas,
the happier, healthier, and more
financially independent you will be.*
- - John Wolcott Adams,

Power Words For Prosperous Living

Introduction . . .

THIS book was written especially for YOU and everyone who loves prosperity and wants to enjoy more of it. My intention in producing this publication is to give you powerful tool that helps you acquire and maintain a healthy, prosperous attitude of mind, and condition, on a daily basis. Reading just a page-a-day--about one minute--will empower you to PRO$PER NOW!

Russell H. Conwell said in his famous *Acres of Diamonds* lectures, "I say you ought to be rich; you have no right to be poor. To live and not be rich is a misfortune and it is doubly a misfortune because you could have been rich just as well as being poor."

RICH is having an abundance of good, living a full, abundant, comfortable life.
PROSPER means to flourish, succeed, and thrive.
NOW means presently, today, forthwith, no waiting.
$ is a combination of H and S symbolizing the Holy Spirit. Therefore, money is spiritual, God's idea of increase, and a handy medium of exchange.

Prosperity, of course, is more than just having lots of money, as good and wonderful as that is. It is having an intimate realization of, and connection with, the spiritual source of all wealth.

1

While the emphasis of this book is on empowering you to be financially well-off, keep in mind that true prosperity is being wealthy in peace of mind, love, friendships, health and happiness. Most of all, it is having a deep, abiding relationship with the presence of God within you.

Jim Rosemergy, in his excellent book, *Even Mystics Have Bill To Pay,* said that the key to being truly prosperous is in knowing that God is your Source, and a consciousness of God is your supply. In other words, it is having such an intimate relationship with God, the Source of all wealth, that it flows out through you and positively influences all your activities. Then you have a solid spiritual foundation under your prosperity that creates the consciousness of, and fills your life with, the abundant love, beauty, goodness, and magnificence of God.

As simple as the inspirations on the pages of this book may seem, do not underestimate the power of the ideas contained in them. As you read, it will be helpful for you to quietly "tune in" and listen for the guidance Spirit has for you.

Remember that love is the most important thing of all. Make love the foundation of your prosperity and it will fulfill your desire for riches in a grand way. In my book, *Be What You Are: Love,* I wrote: "The imperative thing for life, for freedom and peace, is love. Love is life. Love is Light. Love is all there is. *The golden key is focusing your attention upon love. Love is the golden answer to everything. Love is life and what you are.*"

Symbology of the Heart and Butterfly on the cover of this book: It is love that moves in the caterpillar as the metamorphosing energy that causes it to be transformed into a beautiful, free-flying butterfly. The same is true for you, as I discovered this for myself many years ago. Consciously and deliberately allow love to be the moving force of your prosperity and you will fly free into the rich abundance God has for you. Through love you will claim and enjoy the millions that are yours by divine right.

Again, it is divinely right for you to be just as prosperous as possible, *now, today!* Reading this book daily as intended--just a-one-minute-page-a-day-- will enable you to enjoy your rich inheritance as a deserving child of God. Thus you open the floodgates of infinite plenty and you enjoy the vast rich good awaiting your acceptance of it. In every wonderful way, you will PRO$PER NOW!

3

Most of these Prosperity Inspirations and Prayers may be found on my website: GoldenKeyMinistry.com. However, they may vary from those in this handy book. Keep a copy on your desk, night stand, coffee table, and other convenient places for quick reference and daily inspiration. This will help you travel the royal road to riches, to enjoy the trip, and improve the quality of your life. Invite friends and associates to join you and together, use this book as your daily prosperity guide. Please write and tell me how this book is helping you to *Pro$per Now!*

John Wolcott Adams
P. O. Box 30989
Phoenix, AZ 85046-0989 USA
RevJohn@GoldenKeyMinistry.com

When you hold in your mind an active, alive and clear picture of what you desire, and know within yourself that it is already yours, it's a done deal! Nothing can prevent it from coming to you.

- - John Wolcott Adams,
"How I Can Have Everything"

PRO$PER NOW! #1

PEOPLE who are wise, who are clear in their desire for true, overflowing prosperity, and who have learned to use prospering words, spend at least a few minutes in daily scientific prayer speaking *Power Words for Prosperous Living.* They know, prosperity affirmations build prosperity consciousness, which in turn expresses in prosperous conditions.

Prosperous thinking always precedes prosperous living. To affect a change in your manifest prosperity, change your thinking first. It may not always be easy to do, but begin and persist, and you will see welcomed changes taking place in your prosperity that will affect every area of your life.

Prosperity Prayer: Through the power of my thought and word, prospering changes are happening in me and in my life now.

PRO$PER NOW! #2

WHEN faced with apparent financial lack, it is essential that you look beyond the appearance and see with your mind and heart, the abundance of God. This is the time to affirm and to know the Truth: God in you is both the Giver and the Gift. Let go of all fear. Choose now which you will serve, Fear or Faith. Fear compounds the apparent lack. Faith dissolves it and brings forth what you need, and much more.

Remember that God wants you to live prosperously. When you focus your faith on Him and His rich supply, you open the way for it to pour more freely into your life.

Prosperity Prayer: In faith, I know that God is prospering me richly and abundantly now.

PRO$PER NOW! #3

DO YOU have all the prosperity you really desire? Have you opened your mind wide enough to God's vast good for you? Are you allowing His rich treasure to manifest in your life? If not, why not?

Jesus said, "It is your Father's good pleasure to GIVE you the kingdom." If that is true, and it is, why don't more people take Him at His word and accept ALL of the good God has for them?

God's abundance is everywhere present for every one. It is okay for you to accept a much larger share than you have claimed so far. Go ahead and do it now!

Prosperity Prayer: It is my Father's good pleasure to give me His treasure in marvelous measure.

PRO$PER NOW! #4

Catherine Ponder told of a man who went to Florida to get in on a boom, but the boom burst about the time he arrived and he was soon in bad financial shape. Fortunately, he learned that he could tithe his way to prosperity and decided to try it.

The first year his income increased 60%. The next year it increased 100%. He continued to tithe and he became the owner of some of the largest real estate companies in the state. His income escalated into the millions! He taught the tithing law of prosperity to one of his associates who was in debt and he too was soon debt-free, plus he had a sizable bank account. Later he went into business for himself and became exceedingly financially prosperous.

Prosperity Prayer: I no longer strain and strive, I tithe and thrive!

PRO$PER NOW! #5

WE LIVE in an exceedingly rich universe in which all that is needed for our daily provision is at hand. All that we could possibly need is already provided, yet we tend to work very hard to make it a reality in our lives.

What we need to do is to get still, mentally and spiritually, absorbing, receiving, this infinite abundance into our minds. Feel our oneness with it, and then invite it to manifest as our daily bread.

E. V. Ingraham wrote: "By prayer, breathe in the greatness, the grandeur, the nearness of God. All the universe is your storehouse from which to receive."

Prosperity Prayer: **My supply is at hand. It fills me, thrills me, surrounds me, and prospers me now!**

PRO$PER NOW! #6

THERE must be balance in giving and receiving. It is not enough to just give or to just receive. Giving keeps substance in circulation and receiving does the same thing. Too often, it is believed that God's supply for an individual is very limited when, in truth, it is not.

Open your mind to the vast abundance of the Universe, accept it as yours, claim your oneness with it, believe you are receiving, and act as though you really consider it as true. Do this religiously on a daily basis and you will see your prosperity grow in amazing ways! That is the intention of these daily PRO$PER NOW inspirations.

Prosperity Prayer: My mind is open to, and I am one with, the vast abundance of the Universe. My prosperity is growing in amazing ways now!

PRO$PER NOW! #7

IT IS always good to practice the Gratitude Attitude in prayer. Be grateful for what you expect and give thanks again when it manifests. In that way, your life becomes more positive and fulfilled and your prosperity grows in wonderful ways. By thanking God for answered prayer, before and after receiving, you align yourself with the Great Affirmative.

Believe you receive what you affirm (pray) for and joyfully thank God for that or something better. A person, who had experienced financial difficulties, began to thank God for abundance in the face of negative appearances. Everywhere he went, he continually gave thanks for whatever happened, or came to him. Within a few days, he miraculously received several thousand dollars!

Prosperity Prayer: Thank You God, for the abundance now manifesting in my life in amazing ways. I prosper now!

TOO many people, after setting their goals, allow themselves to be stopped by adversity or they accept something less. They believe that is all they are worth, which is not true. You live in a fabulously rich Universe that desires for you to claim and accept your rich inheritance.

The Universe always has more for you, not less. If you settle for less, you may as well admit to yourself that settling for less was your intended goal! Always set your goals high, but within reach, with effort. By putting forth the right amount of energy and effort, you will have that, or something better! Never be stopped by adversity.

Never give up just because things may not be going well. By persisting, you will be successful provided you are doing your inner and outer work and your goals are worthwhile.

Prosperity Prayer: I give thanks for God's unfailing help as I persist. My success and prosperity are assured.

W. Clement Stone wrote: "Psychological researchers, ministers, and self-made businessmen came to the same conclusion: We are poor or rich not because God ordained it, but because of the way in which we use the talent and abilities given to us by God!"

S. B. Fuller, who made it big in spite of beginning in a poverty environment. His mother told him, "We are poor, not because of God, but because we have not developed a desire to be rich!" He decided to be rich. He sold soap door to door, saved up $25,000. Borrowed another $125,000, bought the company he worked for and went on to own several companies and a newspaper.

This happened many years ago but the same attitude is true today and will work for you. Prosperity begins with desire! It is achieved through a Positive Mental Attitude!

Prosperity Prayer: My desire to be rich, and my Positive Mental Attitude produce marvelous abundance for me now!

PRO$PER NOW! #10

A YOUNG MAN seemed to lack many of the qualities that would assure success in his chosen field, but he was well endowed with persistence. He experienced many put downs, and his faith was tested over and over. He sometimes wondered why his prosperity was seemingly kept from him, about his apparent inadequacy and lack of self-worth. He wondered too, if success would ever come to him. But, he kept his goals in sight and his faith strong as he persisted.

Eventually, his prosperity began to grow. Failure gave way to success and because he persisted, he became very happy, prosperous and successful. Put the golden key of persistence to work in your life. Don't allow yourself to think small. Think BIG. Think prosperously, and persist, and you will be amazed at how your prosperity grows in delightful ways.

Prosperity Prayer: Thinking prosperously, I persist toward my goals and my prosperity grows and grows!

PRO$PER NOW!   #11

SPEAKING in a kind and loving way toward the Source of your supply will enhance your prosperity It is not because it matters to God, but because you attract what you are. If a person rails against God, that is, gripes, whines, complains to God about his apparently meager supply, he creates obstacles that deter God's riches from manifesting in his life.   Griping, whining and complaining are out of harmony with spiritual law.

Loving kindness is expressed by those who know they are divine beings, the emissaries of God, through which God gives His good to others. Loving kindness can be big acts, but are more often, small ones. It is easier to do small, kind and loving things for other people. Loving kindness is a golden key to prosperity . . . *Your* prosperity!

Prosperity Prayer: With Love as my guide, I happily act in kind and loving ways. Love is my golden key to prosperity!

PRO$PER NOW! #12

ASK yourself: "What would I desire if there were no limitations or restrictions and I was sure the universe would definitely give it to me?" It might be something you have already decided upon, but for this purpose, pick something else, something big and wonderful! Most people think too small, so really stretch your thinking and imagination. Think BIG! Do not be concerned with HOW it will come about. After you have written down your desire, ask yourself this question: "Is this the best I can do?"

Probably, you can do better. Remember that the Universe can give you whatever you ask. So allow your mind to expand into greater dimensions and possibilities. Why can you have what you ask for? The answer is W.G.A.T.A.P. With God All Things Are Possible. It may seem impossible to you, but with God, it's a piece of cake! So, get with God and Prosper Now!

Prosperity Prayer: With God, I now move forward into my expanded good, divinely directed. I prosper now!

PRO$PER NOW! #13

IN YOUR quest to prosper in all areas of life, and in the highest and best way, it is essential to put God first. That is because God is Love. Love is the fulfilling substance of everything worthwhile which you may desire to achieve, have, do, or be.

We all enjoy spurts of prosperity, but it is so much better to experience permanent, ever-increasing prosperity that does not diminish or go away. Prosperous thinking people are never satisfied with low level or temporary prosperity, especially in the light of having a very loving and rich Father Who desires, more than anything, to bestow His riches upon His children.

Establish yourself in permanent prosperity by accepting that God is your source and your consciousness of God is your supply. God is love, and He loves to prosper you.

Prosperity Prayer: **God is my Source and my Prosperity. God's rich supply comes to me through His own wonderful channels now.**

17

IS a financial matter causing you worry? Release it to God. Stop thinking about it, at least in an anxious way. Refocus your thinking upon what you have and the prosperity increase you desire. Golden Key the matter by thinking and declaring . . . *I have!*

Another way to turn the Golden Key, when suffering a lack attack, is to visit places where there is an abundance of things such as furniture, food, etc. Also go to a high vantage point where you can see for miles, or go outside at night and look at the billions of stars in the sky. Declare and accept that all of this is yours. It is God's gift to you. Let it give you the feeling of being exceedingly prosperous. There's always more than enough for you.

Prosperity Prayer: Thinking prosperously, I turn away from lack and limitation. Thinking prosperously, I claim and accept the infinite riches God has for me now.

PRO$PER NOW! #15

A LARGE inhibitor of enhanced prosperity is Fear, and it needs to be dealt with. Some people are afraid to *really ask* for more and better. Other people are fearful of actually letting go and allowing their spiritual potential to be expressed more beautifully and productively. Still others seem to be locked into very limited concepts of themselves so that they are unable to see a higher way of life. Consequently, fear keeps them in bondage to the lesser, when they could just as well have more and better.

I wrote in my book, *Be What You Are: Love,* Every negative in your life, sickness, anger, frustration, lack of money, inharmonious relationships, are the appearance of fear. Yet, fear has no reality. Love lets you be free from fear. Love frees you to prosper. Love will enhance your prosperity like nothing else.

Prosperity Prayer: Love prospers me now. All channels are open and free, and God's vast rich good now comes to me!

PRO$PER NOW! #16

ASK YOURSELF: "Is what I am thinking, feeling, saying, and doing, enhancing my prosperity? Is there room for improvement?" If so, here are some helpful reminders for enhancing your prosperity:

1. Refrain from all lack-thinking. Think and speak. . . *I have!*
2. Refrain from all criticism, condemnation, and complaining.
3. Be optimistic. Expect the Best!
4. Tithe faithfully and joyfully.
5. Do not be negative about anything. Think, speak in an upward manner.
6. Accept. Accept your desires as yours now.
7. Give a Faith-Offering in expectation of receiving.
8. Give thanks just as though all your dreams have already come true.
9. Relax, let go, and let God prosper you now.

Prosperity Prayer: I keep my thoughts uplifted, happy, loving, positive, and prospering.

PRO$PER NOW! #17

YOU may be busy with every day work and other activities, but while you are, keep your mind open to prospering ideas. Look for ways to help and to prosper other people. But be alert to the infinite opportunities to become rich, or richer.

There is a Gold Mine within you just waiting, as-it-were, to be mined by you. Too often we are too busy outwardly, and forget or neglect to really search within--to go directly to the Source. To have more prosperity, go where your prosperity is, within you. Open your mind to prospering ideas. Keep receptive and they will come, often when you are relaxed or doing something else. When they do, entertain them royally and they will prosper you.

Prosperity Prayer: Seeking within, I discover the Gold Mine of prospering ideas in me, and they prosper me now!

ALL that the Universe has, is really yours. You have every right to claim your share, which is so abundant you cannot possibly comprehend it all. Do not fear taking anything from anyone else because there is more than enough for everyone.

Simply make sure you claim your inheritance from the Universe and not from the world or people. Your inheritance, as a child of God is yours now, not at some future time, unless you prefer to put off receiving it. The Universe is God, the Father within, the Source of your supply.

In faith, claim your inheritance by getting very still, unifying with it in thought and feeling, and accepting its rich provision for you. Then act as though you believe this is true. Go forth in confidence, faith, peace, and expectancy.

Prosperity Prayer: **As the deserving child of a wealthy Father, I now claim and accept my inheritance of unlimited wealth.**

RICH IDEAS make you R .B. M. - Rich Beyond Measure, a preferable way to be. Most people struggle to make it financially, but do not prosper to the degree they would like to experience. That is because they fail to seek within, opening their minds to rich ideas.

Rich ideas, when put to work prospered Henry Ford, Walter P. Chrysler, Andrew Carnegie, Bill Gates, Luther Burbank, Don Brown, and many other wealthy men. Prospering ideas have been born into the consciousness of people who have used them to benefit not just themselves, but millions of people.

All the rich ideas have not yet been used up. They are infinite and right where you are now. Ask and you will receive!

Prosperity Prayer: Seeking within, rich ideas are revealed to me. I put them to work, and I prosper richly and abundantly now.

PRO$PER NOW!   #20

A YOUNG MAN, who, after many years of living in financial lack, finally made a commitment to really live the prosperous life he was sure God wanted him to live. He dedicated himself to doing everything he could to make himself and his loved ones really happy and prosperous. It wasn't easy because of so many years of negative, limited thinking, but he did succeed.

Commitment and persistence made him victorious and he became more prosperous and happier than he could have imagined. You can have all you desire by making a commitment to having it and persisting toward your goal. You can be just as prosperous as you really desire.

Prosperity Prayer: Divinely guided, I dedicate myself to thinking, speaking, and living prosperously now.

PRO$PER NOW! #21

THERE is no virtue in being poor and no one has the right to live in poverty. It is a disease that must be healed. The way to heal it is to get rich! Prosperity doesn't mean the same thing to everyone yet most people equate prosperity to having plenty of money. There is nothing wrong with having financial abundance, when it is done with integrity.

Jesus, the Great Prosperity Teach, never sanctioned poverty. He promoted prosperity. Money, of itself, does not make a person wealthy, but it is a whole lot easier to be happy and healthy with plenty of money, especially when it comes to you honestly. The Truth is, God wants you to have plenty. So, accept that it is divinely right for you to be financially prosperous, and step into the mainstream of universal supply.

Prosperity Prayer: I am in the mainstream of universal supply. I accept my divine right to prosper in the way God wants me to, and I do!

ARE YOU suffering from the P. L. O. M disease? It is contagious and can actually be fatal? P. L. O. M stands for 'Poor Little Old Me.' When you engage in that kind of thinking, which is feeling sorry for yourself because of focusing on what you apparently lack, you tend to make your world a miserable place.

If on the other hand, you count your blessings and look at your fellow humans, it is possible that you are better off than many people.

A better idea is H. G. I. A. Instead of poor little old me, change your thinking to 'How Great I Am. By changing your thoughts and feelings, looking on the bright side and focusing on abundance, serves to lift you onto a higher, more prospering level.

Prosperity Prayer: Looking on the bright side, I realize How Great I Am. God made me this way and prospers me richly!

PRO$PER NOW! #23

A PERSON who read my book, *How To Have 'Unexpected' Income*, wrote to say that some very exciting things were happening in her life. One of them, she was given a gift of $50,000!

Now, if she can do that, so can you. God does not limit His rich provision to only a select few of His children. His abundance is available for everyone. If you do not yet have the prosperity you really desire, have you opened your mind enough to God's vast good for you? Are you allowing His rich treasure to come into your life through unexpected channels?

The golden key to unlimited prosperity is opening your mind to all of God's rich good. This means to open it wider than ever before, and invite abundance to flow into your life. Keep doing this and the prosperity floodgates will open and your richer prosperity will flow more freely for you.

Prosperity Prayer: **My mind is open, I am receptive, and God's vast rich good is now pouring freely into my life.**

27

THERE are no two ways about it. If you desire to live the more abundant life, if you desire to be truly happy, healthy, and prosperous, (and you should) love is the bottom line. It is also the top line and all lines in between.

When Paul said that love is the fulfilling of the law, he knew what he was talking about. He had learned through hard experience that trying to do things without love was not only fruitless, but detrimental to his health.

When Jesus said that love is the greatest commandment, He knew this was true because of His deep inner connection with God. He knew that love is the real power for happy, successful living. It is still true today. Love is the only power that will truly prosper you in every desirable way.

Prosperity Prayer: Love is the way. Love is now prospering me in every wonderful way, and I am grateful.

PRO$PER NOW! #25

WHAT you hold in mind makes your rich or poor. Wrong thoughts tend toward poverty; right thoughts tend toward prosperity. Regardless of your present condition, there is always room for improvement. In your imagination, hold yourself in abundant prosperity. As you continue doing this, you set in motion the forces that will sooner or later bring you into a much greater and more desirable condition.

Regardless of adversity, do not allow yourself to be depressed. Lift up your head in faith and do the best you can with what you have in the faith that things are getting better. By holding yourself in this attitude, you radiate strong, positive energy that literally attracts to you, prospering power and substance. To have a Prosperous Future depends upon your practice of a Prosperous NOW.

Prosperity Prayer: Thank You God, for my growing rich consciousness and for unlimited riches in my life now.

HERE is something that will help you enjoy greater prosperity. Deliberately cause yourself to think and feel prosperous. Think, speak, and act as though you are already fabulously rich. (In truth, you are!) You have all of God's rich substance within you and surrounding and enfolding you every moment. Believe with unwavering faith that God is your instant, constant, and abundant source of supply. (Financial and otherwise.)

Upon awakening each morning, think about God and His abundance. Then let this be your last thought as you drift off to sleep at night. Go to sleep happy in the Truth that you live in God's universe of fabulous plenty in which all your needs are met, and your loving Father's rich abundance is flowing freely into your life. Be deeply grateful for this new reality.

Prosperity Prayer: Thank You God, for Your living substance prospering me richly and abundantly now. I am grateful!

PRO$PER NOW! #27

WHEN F. W. Woolworth started his first five and dime store, it was very small and people said it would fail. He proved them wrong. He was the one with the seed-idea and the faith. From that store seed-idea, grew a business of immense proportions.

Jesus said, 'When you pray, believe you receive." He was stating a powerful prosperity principle and action of Mind. He knew that everything is done by faith. He also said to have the faith of a tiny grain of mustard seed. What He was really saying to you and me is, we are to do as the mustard seed when planted in fertile soil.

Seeds don't question, doubt, or have qualms about what will happen. Nor do they give energy to unworthiness or worry about past mistakes. They do what they are designed to do. Plant your prosperity seeds in Mind, believe in the process, and enjoy being prospered now.

Prosperity Prayer: I plant my prosperity seeds because I know, God's riches for me grow.

PRO$PER NOW! #28

IT IS not enough for you to only be financially prosperous. If you seek financial wealth alone, you will be disappointed. It is good to have plenty of money, much better than the alternative. But what good is plenty of money if you do not have love, are unhappy, lack peace of mind, or have no true friends who love you for who you are.

I know a person who is quite wealthy, financially, but who is not balanced in other areas and has few real friends. In your quest for prosperity, make sure that it is well-rounded. Someone once said that peace of mind is to be sought after first and foremost. It's important to be prosperous in all areas of life, and to remember that love is the most important thing of all. Then you have balanced prosperity.

Prosperity Prayer: God is Love, the Source of my supply. I give thanks for ever-increasing prosperity in all areas of my life now.

IT SEEMS that in getting caught up in daily activity, or in the appearance of lack, we sometimes forget that supply is limitless. Regardless of what it is, that which has been produced, can be reproduced.

Keep this in mind, especially when your money supply appears to be running low. Instead of saying, "I am running out of money," say, "It is time for a refilling of my money supply from the unlimited storehouse of Infinite Spirit!"

Do this, of course, while looking to God for the replenishing of your supply and not to other people. God is your Source, not people. In faith, seek your own directly from the inexhaustible Source within you, and it will be provided.

Prosperity Prayer: In faith, I seek my own. God is constantly refilling my money supply, and I am grateful!

ONE time, someone broke into my home and took several hundred dollars worth of camera equipment, and other items. I admit, it took me a while to really forgive that person, and to realize that he had a much bigger problem than I did.

For a while, I gave in to feelings of loss, anger, and wanting to punish him. Remembering that God is my source, I realized there were other cameras and God would provide me with a replacement. Then I blessed and forgive that person. I was even grateful for the vacuum so the Universe could fill it with something better. Soon, I was given a new, much better camera that still takes excellent pictures. When there appears to be loss, let it go as you remember that God is your Source. Forgiveness always opens the door of greater prosperity for you.

Prosperity Prayer: **Forgiving and letting go, I trust God to increase my prosperity in His own wonderful way. I prosper now!**

DO EVERYTHING you can to alleviate all lack from your consciousness and your life by affirming and claiming the rich abundance God has for you. Use the mighty power of your spoken word. If you could measure this power, you would be amazed, but there is a good way to see just how mighty it is.

Every day, pray affirmative prosperity prayers such as are shared with you through this book, with feeling and acceptance. This is scientific prayer and it always works. You will, in due time, see wonderful changes come about. First they will come in your thinking and attitude and then manifest as increased practical prosperity. Doing this will empower you to prosper in all ways.

Prosperity Prayer: In faith and confidence I affirm and claim God's rich abundance and I prosper now! Thank you God, I am grateful!

PRO$PER NOW! #32

IF YOU do not fully believe and accept that the Universe wants you to both live splendidly and demonstrate accordingly, you have the power to change your thinking. True prosperity absolutely includes the demonstration of right living conditions, right activity, and genuine happiness.

Right living conditions means to be beautifully clothed, housed, and transported in the manner that makes you feel best. You can demonstrate these circumstances through the use of your own mind power according to the spiritual laws and principles that govern true prosperity. Accept your divine right to live splendidly now. (From the author's book, *How To Have 'Unexpected' Income.*)

Prosperity Prayer: **Living splendidly is my divine right and I do it now!**

RIGHT activity is wholesome and positive, and never harms anyone. It benefits all who may be affected in any way. Through right activity, you empower others to benefit, directly and indirectly, by your actions.

Genuine happiness comes through getting in touch with the real energy of right living conditions and activity. That energy is love and empowers you to live life lovingly, happily, and prosperously. (From the author's book, *How To Have 'Unexpected' Income*)

Right activity in relation to prosperity gives you peace of mind, and it benefits countless other people, too. And, it comes back to you, *multiplied!*

Prosperity Prayer: Divinely guided, I do things right and my prosperity is happy and bright!

BY putting lots of love into all you do, you build a solid foundation under your activity which results in true happiness--the kind that wells up from deep within you and spills over into the lives of others.

Loved ones, friends, coworkers, and business associates will benefit along with you when you put lots of love into your prospering activity. Love is the essence of true prosperity and brings joy in accomplishment. It just makes you feel good all over!

Love prospers you like nothing else can or ever will! Love opens the doors and windows of abundance and it inundates your life with all the rich blessings of God.

Prosperity Prayer: Thankfully, and I know it's true, Love prospers me richly in everything I do!

PRO$PER NOW! #35

A MAN awakened one day to the fact that life was not very exciting or satisfying. He had struggled, sometimes in questionable ways, to make a living but he finally saw the light, he wisely decided to change his ways.

He sought teachers and books from which to learn and was surprised at how things began to change.

He learned that God is the source of his supply, he began to love himself as he let go of old thinking and behavior patterns.

His prosperity grew in wonderful ways and he enjoyed happiness he had only dreamed of before. Now he knows what it is to be truly prosperous, and his life is now exciting and happy.

Prosperity Prayer: Letting go of old ways, I now enjoy happy, prospering days!

M. I. E. stands for Mind, Idea, Expression. It is the basic law of manifestation. First in mind, the idea, then the expression of the idea, much like a sculptor sees the statue in a block of stone, or an artist sees the finished picture before beginning to paint.

Imagination and faith work together in putting on canvas, what the painter sees in his mind's eye while letting his fingers and brush to the work. So it is with the prosperous life you desire. Hold a steady picture in your imagination of your desired prosperity, pour in lots of faith, and then let it manifest, which it surely will.

In this way, you create in your mind, the mental equivalent of your rich, prosperous life.

Prosperity Prayer: In my imagination, I see my increased prosperity. Through my faith in God, the Source, it manifests for me now.

PRO$PER NOW! #37

WOULD you like more prosperity in your home? Then take to heart these words of Myrtle Fillmore, cofounder of Unity. "You can begin now to bring more prosperity into your home. The first thing for you to do is to discard the words that have in them the idea of poverty, and then select carefully the words that hold the idea of plenty."

To put it simply, choose carefully the words you speak. No longer use words that imply financial lack or limitation. Discipline yourself to speak only prospering, uplifting words. Invite your family to join with you in this activity. It will fill your home with positive energy that attracts prospering substance. Soon you will experience more prosperity in your home. It works in business places, too.

Prosperity Prayer: I choose to speak only prospering, uplifting words, and I prosper now in God's amazing ways.

PRO$PER NOW!   #38

IT IS important to affirm and accept that God is prospering YOU. While you surely want others to be blessed, it is vital to focus on receiving God's blessings for yourself as well.

This is emphasized because many people are hesitant to accept more prosperity for themselves. Such reluctance may stem from old beliefs of not deserving more, or limited concepts of what they need or want. Also, they sometimes believe other people are worthier.

While desiring that everyone prosper, you certainly do not want your good to pass you by, so affirm and accept that you deserve ALL the rich good God has for you. Gratefully claim and accept it now.

Prosperity Prayer: **Gratefully, I claim and accept ALL of the rich good God has for me, and I prosper now!**

PRO$PER NOW! #39

A POSITIVE, prosperous future depends upon positive, prosperous beliefs and actions *now*. Today, do your best with what you have to work with. Give thanks for it and have great expectations of God's highest good for you.

It is wise to set goals and to write them on paper because that is a prerequisite to a happy, productive, and prosperous life. Once you write out your goals, live in them in your mind now, not in the future, but as if they are already yours now. Put your faith completely in God, the Source, and have great expectations. Believe you receive, and that you are prospering more abundantly, now!

Prosperity Prayer: I keep my beliefs positive and prospering. With faith in God, the Source, I have great expectations. I AM prospering richly and abundantly now!

FAITH is essential to success. You must have faith in yourself, in God in you, and in what your are doing. Faith is believing, without doubting, that you will succeed even when appearances may sometimes seem to tell you differently.

When there seems to be no way, faith is knowing there IS a way. God always opens the way when you keep your faith strong and securely grounded in Him, and have great expectations. If you are expecting greater prosperity, then expect it greatly with complete faith. Give thanks just as though you have it *now*. There are no delays in God, neither are there delays in you. God is always on time. The time is *now*.

Prosperity Prayer: With faith in God, myself, and my goals, I give thanks for perfect results, and I prosper now!

PRO$PER NOW! #41

IT SEEMS paradoxical that with so much abundance in the world, so many people still struggle to prosper. In some parts of the world, millions of people live in poverty.

While you should strive for peace, prosperity must be given high priority because it is extremely difficult for anyone to be at peace while worrying and struggling for adequate food, clothing, and shelter.

Collectively, we must do all we can to help everyone to prosper--to abound in plenty, and be happy and healthy, wanting for nothing. Individually, we should do all we can to prosper because what we do for ourselves, we do for everyone. When we are prosperous, we radiate high energy that blesses all.

Prosperity Prayer: **Divinely guided, I am moving quickly and easily into my wonderful new prosperous life. I prosper now!**

PRO$PER NOW! #42

BRAD JENSEN wrote: "You are wealthy now with an abundance of what you are thinking about. The world is a creative engine, and will create whatever you are really thinking. Every thought in your mind is a prayer about you, no matter who the subject seems to be.

"The only way to manifest lack is to hold something against someone else. Give up all thoughts of offense, revenge, of being injured, of self-justification, of needing to defend yourself against others' expectations, of unfairness of life, of others getting some unearned good fortune, think 'Good for them! God is blessing and prospering them and I bless them also!'"

Prosperity Prayer: Letting go of every negative, unforgiving thought. I think the best, and I am wealthy now!

PRO$PER NOW! #43

IN THE appearance of lack, declare over and over: "Thank You God, for the abundance that is mine." Do this until your whole being resonates with God's abundance. This will drive lack out of your consciousness and cause abundance to take its place in your mind and in your life.

With no job, a woman did this when she didn't know where food or money were to come from for herself and her small children. She practiced being thankful, making this declaration over and over. Whatever happened, she said, "Thank You, God." When she received even small blessings, she declared, "Thank You, God." Before long, she was led to a good company where she was truly appreciated and well-paid. Everything substantially improved as she kept declaring, "Thank You, God, for the abundance that is mine!"

Prosperity Prayer: Thank You God, for the abundance that is mine I prosper now!

47

PRO$PER NOW! #44

AN IMPORTANT point to consider is your love for prosperity. It may seem odd, but some people do not love prosperity. They somehow believe that it is wrong to have plenty. This may be due to a belief that to live abundantly -- to have plenty of money -- is not spiritual, or that they are unworthy of the riches of God.

To prosper means to succeed, to flourish, and to thrive. Therefore, everyone should love to prosper because that is the way God wants for all of His children to live. Jesus, the Great Prosperity Teacher, taught and demonstrated prosperity. We are here to live more abundant lives. To do anything less is to go against the natural universal flow of prosperity. The Universe is abundant with every possibility. Our part is to get in the flow and love to prosper.

Prosperity Prayer: I love prosperity. I love to prosper, and I prosper now!

PRO$PER NOW! #45

LOVE is an integral part of prosperous living. When love is genuinely felt and expressed, it is never done for show or to impress others. Love is caring and sharing, and being patient, kind, and understanding.

While some financially wealthy people may flaunt their riches and status, there are those who unselfishly live life lovingly with the welfare of their fellow humans first in their hearts.

Love all people, beginning with yourself. In so doing you are loving God because you are an expression of Him. Thus you open the way for God to prosper you more abundantly.

Prosperity Prayer: Loving God, all people, and myself, I live life lovingly and prosperously now!

PRO$PER NOW! #46

A WOMAN struggled for years under a load of guilt believing that because of things she had done, she was not worthy of, and therefore, not entitled to prosper.

When helped to understand that God (Love) does not keep track of wrongs, she decided to fully and completely forgive herself, especially for denying God the opportunity to prosper her.

Loving herself unconditionally, she freely loved everything and everybody in the same way. Love made of her an irerestible magnet. Soon, prosperity miracles began happening to her. When you love yourself in this way, prosperity miracles happening to you, too!

Prosperity Prayer: I love myself and all people unconditionally, and prosperity miracles are happening to me now!

*BRAD JENSEN, an enormously blessed man, wrote: "Let go of what you aren't really using. If you are holding on to something (person, place, or thing - or even an idea) because you think you might need it later, you are really telling yourself that you do not own that thing, you do not deserve it, and you do not believe you can recreate it in the future.

"These are all poverty thoughts. Clean out your closets, have a garage sale or give to Goodwill, but let go of all that spiritual cholesterol that is clogging your arteries of good."

Prosperity Prayer: Cleaning up and cleaning out, I let it go and move into my greater prosperity now.

*Brad Jensen: www.elstore.com

PRO$PER NOW! #48

PROSPEROUS THINKING PAYS! A businessman was over $800,000 in debt when he opened his mind to prosperous thinking. Through using prosperity prayers, and the acceptance of prospering ideas, he planted seeds of prosperity and freedom. He opened his mind to prospering ideas and opportunties. Shortly, he began to prosper, earning over $200,000 a year, and was soon out of debt and enjoying his financial freedom.

Open your mind to the uplifting, prospering power and ideas within you. Allow this great energy to more freely express itself through your thinking. You will be amazed at what happens!

Prosperity Prayer: My mind is open to prospering ideas. Thinking prosperously, I prosper in amazing ways now!

GOD IS ADEQUATE! Dr. Emma Smiley wrote in her book, *The Bread of Life,* "We do not tithe that we may prosper but to nourish our consciousness, that we may daily become more aware of the Presence of God, that we may the better know the great truth on which all prosperity is based: God is Adequate to Provide All That we Need, Whether Much or Little. This knowing, this awareness, is true prosperity."

God is adequate to provide for all your needs and desires. When you desire to know God with all your heart, and do know Him, you have no needs. They are fulfilled.

Prosperity Prayer: God is adequate to provide all that I need, and desire. Knowing this is true, I prosper now!

PRO$PER NOW! #50

SOME people attract prosperity, but it doesn't stay with them. That is often because they are distracted by guilt, fear, and worry, or perhaps, it is old lack programming. Some people have deep-seated beliefs that it is wrong for them to be prosperous while others have done their homework in creating a solid spiritual foundation for their prosperity to rest upon.

Denying yourself of increased good is denying God the privilege of prospering you. Never object to or refuse financial and other blessings that come to you. Firmly establish your prosperous life in the spiritual Source of wealth. Then, when prosperity blessings come to you, welcome and accept them thankfully!

Prosperity Prayer: I welcome and accept all the prosperity blessings now coming my way. Thank You God!

A HOUSEWIFE was unhappy but didn't know what to do about it. Finally, fed up with a seemingly unappreciative husband and children, work that was drudgery, and an unfulfilled life, she sought ways in which to change things. Soon she came across a book about how her own thoughts and feelings produce her conditions.

Realizing she could change her thinking, she decided to do so. It wasn't easy because the old way of thinking was well-ingrained, but she persisted. She began to love and appreciate herself and to consciously radiate love to other people, starting with her family. The result was like a miracle as her husband and children responded accordingly. Her life became happy, exciting and prosperous!

Prosperity Prayers: I love and appreciate myself and give thanks for my ever-growing prosperity.

ONCE in a while someone will tell me that they are praying *desperately* for their prosperity. I suggest that they never pray *desperately* for anything. True, sometimes there are situations in which fear is a factor and we are anxious to have our prayers answered. However, that kind of fearful attitude usually impedes one's prosperity.

Fear closes your mind so that the natural flow of God's abundance is blocked. On the other hand, love and peace enable you to tap into, and allow the natural flow of prospering substance to move out into your life. To prosper more easily, relax, let go, and be at peace.

Prosperity Prayer: **Relaxing and letting go, I rest in the peaceful assurance that God is prospering me now.**

WOULD you have greater prosperity? Do you desire a more enriching, fulfilling life that is free from petty annoyances, negative influences, financial pressures, and unhappy experiences? How about financial independence? Your golden key to all of this is Love.

Too often a person may spend considerable time and energy in his drive to the top while forgetting the most important thing of all. It is empowering to deliberately allow love to precede and go with you -- to be your prime motivator. Then you leave a trail of beauty, happiness and and kind deeds, and your prosperity is peaceful and wonderful!

Prosperity Prayer: **God is now appearing as me. I love my way and I prosper every day.**

THERE are hundreds of rules for making dreams come true, but four basic rules are as follows:

1. Love your dream.
2. Have faith in your dream.
3. Have faith in yourself and your ability to make it come true.
4. Have a plan of procedure for putting your dream to work.

The first point will give you the least amount of trouble if your dream is not merely an idle wishing, you love it dearly and you want it to come true. The biggest challenge is to get a plan of action that will work. The next essential thing is having faith in yourself and your dream. Quietly draw from the deep reservoir of Divine Love within you, and you will have all you need.

Prosperity Prayer: With faith in myself and in my dreams, love makes my dreams come true.

PRO$PER NOW! #55

A WOMAN who learned of the prosperity law of focusing, and who had tired of a low-paying office job in which she had felt trapped, talked things over with a spiritual counselor. The counselor suggested that she decide on just what she would like to do and to focus on that.

She said that her secret yearning was to sell jewelry and cosmetics. After writing out her desire, she boldly quit her job and stepped out on faith assured that, with God's help, she would be successful. Using the prosperity prayer, below, she went on to achieve outstanding success in the work that brought her great joy and abundant prosperity.

Prosperity Prayer: I am successful now. I am a top salesperson now. With God's help I achieve my goals with ease and I prosper now in God's own wonderful way!

PRO$PER NOW! #56

A MAN who opened a health food store, had some difficulty in getting it to prosper and soon began to experience a lost of enthusiasm for the business. Bills piled up as money seemed to avoid him. Fortunately, he was wise enough to seek the help of a spiritual counselor who talked with him about the spiritual prosperity law of focusing. He also learned to take God as his Partner through tithing.

He focused on his desires, then began praying the prosperity prayer, below. Soon, customers were streaming into his store and gladly buying from him. He became so prosperous, he soon opened another store and that store prospered, too.

Prosperity Prayer: This is God's business and God never fails. I focus my energy upon my goals and with God's help, I am successful in a large and wonderful way now.

PRO$PER NOW! #57

ONE Sunday, Rev. Richard Rogers, senior minister of Unity Church of Phoenix, challenged his listeners to accept all of the good God had for them. He asked if we were really ready and willing to claim that good for ourselves.

Jesus said, "It is your Father's good pleasure to GIVE you the kingdom." The question is, if that is true, why do not more people take Him at his word and accept ALL the good God has for them?

Now, today, is a good time for you to accept a much greater measure of the treasure God has for you. So, do it!

Prosperity Prayer: Right now, today, I claim, accept, and give thanks for ALL of the rich good God has for me. I prosper now!

PRO$PER NOW! #58

CALVIN COOLIDGE offered this gem: "Persistence alone is omnipotent." You may be tested by defeat, but it need not stop you. Think of apparent failure, disappointment, or defeat merely as signposts indicating that success is just around the corner.

Use those signposts to move you forward toward your goal. The way will open, the path will clear and your heart's desires, or something better, will appear. If you do not persist, you will never win the prize. By persisting, you draw forth great power from all over the universe and it comes to move you forward into success and prosperity.

Prosperity Prayer: **Persisting** in faith, all needs are met, all desires of my heart are fulfilled. I prosper now!

PRO$PER NOW!   #59

AN OFFICE worker experienced difficulty getting along with her fellow workers. Everyone seemed to be against her until she examined her own thoughts and feelings. She discovered that she was holding on to little gripes and irritations.

Fortunately, she wised up before the company could fire her. She began loving herself, sending love to her coworkers, and quietly forgave everyone, including herself. Soon there was a change in the people in her office. She wondered about this until she remember that SHE had changed her thinking. She used the following prosperity prayer:

Prosperity Prayer: Love is my real nature. I radiate love. Divine love is my forgiving power and the harmony of this office now. Love mightily prospers me now.

PRO$PER NOW! #60

IT IS GOOD to remember, the Universe only gives you what you are willing to -- and DO accept. Acceptance is a golden key to actually having in your life, the desires of your heart.

Divinely directed, choose your goals and write them on paper. Visualize them clearly in your imagination as yours now. Use prosperity prayers that support your goals. Do all you can to help in the manifestation process, but leave the actual manifestatin to God. That is His job. Let Him do it. Gratefully accept your goals as yours now.

In truth, the desires of your heart are yours now. They are God's gifts to you. Your part is to gratefully accept them.

Prosperity Prayer: God's rich supply is on its way. In love, I gratefully accept mine today!

PRO$PER NOW! #61

IT IS RIGHT, of course, for everyone, especially YOU, to be rich! You should be just as rich as you possibly can. Unfortunately and ignorantly, some people do not believe this due to fear-based religious or parental training.

Regardless of what you may have been taught, God wants you to be rich, to enjoy the happy, prosperous life and to do so in an honest way. You should be financially independent so that you may enjoy the good things money can provide, and because it is divinely right for you to be rich. My friend Jim Melton said, "I've been rich and I've been poor, but rich is better!"

Prosperity Prayer: It is right to be rich. It is right for ME to be rich! God wants me that way. I gratefully accept, and I AM!

ACTUALLY, GOD has everything worked out. He is ready when you are. And, when you are ready, really ready, God's rich good will pour into your life. It may not come as a flood, at first, but come it will! Give thanks for every little bit of improvement and move on with an air of expectancy.

Every thought you think or hold in the Silence, and every word you speak, has some effect upon your subconscious mind and subsequently upon your life. Sometimes it may seem imperceptible but, your thoughts and words do make a difference. So, be impeccably positive and prospering with your word. Don't waste your good mind or word power on negatives. Be mindful to always think and speak prosperously!

Prosperity Prayer: **God is giving, and I'm believing, all His riches, I'm now receiving, and I prosper now!**

PRO$PER NOW! #63

MANY years of counseling experience has taught me that many people do not have a sufficiently high opinion or concept of themselves. This is often true with well-educated people as well as people with much less formal education. Subsequently they tend to work for less because they mistakenly believe they are not worth more.

Fear plays a large part in where a person places himself financially. In order to achieve the kind of success and prosperity you desire, your attitude toward yourself is very important. Take stock of your assets and the positive things about yourself and focus on those. Do not discount yourself. Put yourself up.

Prosperity Prayer: I put myself up. I am the happy, healthy, worthy and wonderful child of God.

PRO$PER NOW! #64

GOD wants you to think highly of yourself and to talk to yourself in positive, prospering, and life-giving words. He wants you to believe in and use your unlimited mind-power for creating within yourself, the consciousness for happy, healthy, and prosperous living. This is the way in which you create the same kind of conditions in your body, life, and affairs.

God wants you to put yourself up because it is difficult to experience the good life while putting yourself down. Never think or talk about yourself in demeaning ways and neither should you ever apologize for yourself. You are a unique creation, a wonderful spiritual being worthy of God's very best!

Prosperity Prayer: I put myself up. I am a wonderful spiritual being worthy of God's very best! I prosper now!

PRO$PER NOW! #65

WHEN you speak positive, healthy, prospering words, you are agreeing with God. You are establishing yourself in the right consciousness that causes God's infinite life, love, wisdom, and substance to flow through you into your life as happy, rich blessings.

Through speaking positive words you establish the "Divine Connection" I wrote about in my book, *Power Words For Prosperous Living!* It is your mind through which the Infinite's riches move into your life. They can come in no other way.

By making the "Divine Connection," through your prospering words, you open the way for more riches to flow into your life.

Prosperity Prayer: I put myself up. I speak only positive, healthy, and prospering words. I prosper now!

PRO$PER NOW! #66

IT IS a known fact that no one should embark upon the achieving of a goal if he does not believe he can achieve that goal. If he starts anyway, he must overcome a very large obstacle that he has placed in his own way.

Believing a goal is attainable helps to generate the enthusiasm needed to get you started in the right attitude and will keep you going once you have taken the first steps.

How much better it is to move in the direction of what you desire to achieve when you believe you can and will achieve your goal. The way is easier, too, and with God's help, it is even more easily achieved.

Prosperity Prayer: **Guided by the light and wisdom of God, I am successful in all that I desire to achieve.**

THOUGHT is creative. You are the product of your own creativity. Changes in your life come about through a new direction of thought. Nothing happens by magic, although some changes may seem magical. No one can really change you but yourself therefore if you look for some thing or person to make immediate changes, you are looking in the wrong direction.

Change always comes from within. A wonderful truth to know is: *You do have the power within to change the circumstances of your life and to call forth the good you desire.*

You can begin right now to make the changes you want and make your life just as prosperous as you really want it to be.

Prosperity Prayer: Thank You God for the power to change my life. I am happy, healthy and prosperous now!

PRO$PER NOW! #68

GOD'S Spirit in you is one of success and prosperity, not failure or lack. God wants you to prosper in all you do. He would not have given you the opportunity to achieve something worthwhile had it been otherwise.

Dr. Emmet Fox said, "Change your mind and keep it changed." He meant that it does little good to change your mind and a few moments, hours, or days later change it back again, to slide back into the old error thinking that has kept you down.

Decide that you will prosper and that is all there is to it. Determine that you will move forward, divinely guided, into your rich new life of joy, happiness, and overflowing prosperity.

Prosperity Prayer: I have decided. My course is set. Divinely guided, I move into my new happy and prosperous life with ease, now!

PRO$PER NOW!   #69

IT IS GOD'S will for you to be fed -- not only with physical food, but with spiritual, emotional, and financial food as well. His intent for you is overflowing abundance of all that is good, not just a little or just enough to get by.

It is not the intention of Infinite Intelligence for you to resign yourself to suffering needlessly (and all suffering is needless). Realize that the vast abundance of the Infinite's riches are available for you, and that you deserve much more than you have claimed so far. Then hold a positive attitude in relation to Him. Claim your share of the unlimited riches God has for all His children. There is plenty for all.

Prosperity Prayer: God's will for me is overflowing abundance. I accept and I give thanks for my expanding prosperity now!

PRO$PER NOW! #70

YOU CAN be more prosperous regardless of your present circumstances. The possibilities and opportunities are limitless. You can enjoy good health and be radiantly and positively alive. You can experience a truly happy and joyous life with warm, loving human relationships.

You can have a truly free, creatively fulfilled and successful life that is independent and unrestrained. If it is money you want, you can have it abundantly! You are the master of your destiny and you guide your personal ship wherever you really want it to go. Think, speak, and act prosperously and you will have your heart's desires. You will sail into the port of infinite plenty!

Prosperity Prayer: Today I think, speak, and act wisely and I move forward into my new life of overflowing prosperity!

74

BRAD JENSEN wrote: "Tithing is giving ten percent of your income to those groups or individuals that you see using spiritual principles in a way that you would like to have grow in your life. Regular, conscious tithing builds your conscious power to accept God's abundance in your life.

"Many churches teach you to tithe to 'your channel of spiritual good.' I say, give where you feel good about giving - where you can give without doubt or restriction. If there is no such place, create one. Give with no strings attached, and receive in the same way."

In a real sense, prosperity is more about giving than about receiving.

Prosperity Prayer: Tithing from my whole income, my life is happy and complete, and I prosper now!

LOOK for ways and opportunities to bless other people; to lend a helping hand even when you receive no apparent remuneration. All that you give in loving service and in material ways, accumulates. Do not be surprised when, down the road a ways, a rather sudden "unexpected" financial blessing is dumped in your lap! It happens all the time and there is no reason why it won't happen to you.

Giving freely of yourself and your wealth, not only blesses others, but creates an open space for you to be richly blessed. This is the way that God gets things done that couldn't be done in any other way. It is love in expression. Especially look for someone to bless today. Then do it!

Prosperity Prayer: I look for opportunities to bless others, and I am richly blessed in God's own wonderful way.

PRO$PER NOW! #73

A COUPLE was experiencing financial difficulties in their business. Their income had taken a serious downturn for no apparent reason, but instead of worrying about the matter, wondering just how they were to pay the rent and other expenses, they daily declared that divine love was working miracles in their financial affairs.

They prayerfully accepted that divine love would provide all the money they needed. After only a few days of doing this, things began to improve and their financial picture got brighter than ever.

Invoke the prospering power of divine love and you will experience financial miracles!

Prosperity Prayer: I am divine love in expression. Divine love is prospering me richly and abundantly now!

ARE you worrying about something? Florence Shinn wrote in her book, *The Game Of Life*, "Why worry, it will probably never happen!" If you worry, it is usually a sign that you are not praying in faith, believing. When you worry, you are believing in and practicing the presence of lack and limitation instead of practicing the presence of God.

A colleague once said that he stopped worrying when he realized that God had created the whole universe without his help!

Worrying is playing old, negative tapes. Erase those tapes and go free. Make prosperous living a happy, enjoyable, wonderful game. Focus on God's rich abundance. He has plenty for you. Relax and gratefully, accept it!

Prosperity Prayer: **Divinely guided, I relax, let go, and let God. Worry-free I play and enjoy the game of prosperous living.**

PRO$PER NOW! #75

Golden Keys To Riches 'n Fun

Focus. There is power when we put our energy behind our ideas . . . Scattered thinking gets scattered results.

Desire. You must have a burning desire for your goal to succeed . . . Desire comes from within.

Commitment. Be willing to do whatever it takes . . . Stick to your idea until it becomes reality.

Persistence. Keep going . . . You can if you think you can.

Enthusiasm. IS contagious . . . Be a carrier!

Key People. Surround yourself with people who are doing the same thing you want to do. Be around wise people and become wise.

Action. Quality action produces results. Live your potential.

Prosperity Prayer: I put to work all of the golden keys to riches 'n fun and I am prospered in every wonderful way now.

ONE DAY, in the early days of Unity School of Practical Christianity, the Sheriff came to repossess some equipment when the Fillmores had gotten behind in their payments. Charles Fillmore, the cofounder, asked him to wait, saying he had a rich Father who would pay what was owed. Upon hearing that, the Sheriff left, satisfied that everything would be okay. Before long, money flowed more freely and everything was paid for easily.

Charles and Myrtle Fillmore had a keen awareness of God as their source regardless of how meager supply seemed to be at times. They held to this belief and were always provided for.

You have the same source and the same supply. Regardless of appearances, believe that God always provides for you.

Prosperity Prayer: **God is my source and I am always abundantly provided for.**

PRO$PER NOW! #77

L-I-D-G-T-T-F-A-T-I-M. A young man who was not doing well financially, learned of this miracle-working formula for prosperity. He pasted these letters in large print up over his bed where he could see them before going to sleep at night. He said that this was his 'open sesame' to a happy, fulfilling and prosperous life.

What do these letters stand for? Lord I Do Give Thee Thanks For The Abundance That Is Mine.

Charles Fillmore wrote, "It has been found by experience that a person increases his blessings by being grateful for what he has. Gratitude even on the mental plane is a great magnet. When gratitude is expressed from a spiritual standpoint it is powerfully augmented."

Prosperity Prayer: Lord I Do Give Thee Thanks For The Abundance That Is Mine.

PRO$PER NOW!   #78

I KNOW a person who continually tells himself, "Things are getting better." His business continues to grow and prosper. Even when there is a little downturn, he says, "Things are getting better." He gives no thought to the downturn. Because he continually feeds his subconscious mind with this and other positive suggestions, his life is continually blessed with ever-increasing success, happiness and prosperity.

Whatever you desire, regardless of appearances, feed your subconscious mind with right ideas and positive information, thus you convince it to produce for you in like kind. Your positive, prospering words have great power upon your subconscious mind, which in turn, draws to you all that is needed to prosper you.

Prosperity Prayer: Things are getting better. I am prospering now!

PRO$PER NOW! #79

ONE time a businesswoman, who was obviously talented in her field, came to talk with me. She was not as successful as she desired to be, and expressed her desire for change. Well-educated, and with many years experience, she felt that she could do better. As we talked, it was discovered that she had quite a limiting belief system which kept her from accepting greater prosperity.

Being intelligent, she quickly realized she must release from her consciousness, old limiting ideas, and replace them with new, prospering ones. This required time and effort, but she persisted and her prosperity began to grow in amazing ways. Now she is enjoying the greater prosperity she had believed God wanted her to have but didn't know how to have it. Now, she does, and so do you!

Prosperity Prayer: **Releasing all lack and limitation, I welcome new, prospering ideas and I am prospered in amazing ways.**

PRO$PER NOW! #80

IT is better to cease all worry and to "Turn the Golden Key," which means to turn away from worries and fears and to focus on God's abundance. Consider this poem by Valerie Hawkins:

WHY?
Why hurry, why sigh;
Why worry, why cry?
Why fret, why stew;
Why make yourself blue"

Why not believe
What you know to be true:
All things worth having
Belong to you!

Worry is an endless circle that begins and ends in the same place. It never produces prosperity. Relax, let go, and let God prosper you.

Prosperity Prayer: Ceasing all worry, I relax and accept all the good God has for me..

PRO$PER NOW! #81

IT PAYS to watch your words. There is a story of a college professor who was berating his students for something. Finally, he said, "If there is a moron in this room, would he or she please stand up?" A few minutes went by and then a fellow in the back of the room, rose slowly to his feet. "Do you mean to tell me, " said the professor, "that you are a moron?" The student hesitated for a moment and then replied, "No, I just hated to see you standing there all by yourself."

Watch your words. To manifest prosperity, do not speak words such as, "I can't afford it," or, "I am poor." Speak words that have in them the idea of plenty such as the prosperity prayer below.

Prosperity Prayer: I live, right now, in the midst of plenty and I am easily prospered. I give thanks for God's rich abundance pouring freely and easily into my life now!

PRO$PER NOW! #82

SOMEONE once said, "It takes a strong constitution to withstand repeated attacks of prosperity." What a nice idea! Too often though, people have repeated "lack attacks." That is because they have given in to the false belief that they are not meant to prosper, or they have a belief system that doesn't allow them to accept the abundance God has for them.

The way to counteract this is to release and let go of every small, limiting thought regarding your prosperity and God's ability to provide for you. Focus on plenty and you will have plenty. Instead of repeated lack attacks, you will have repeated prosperity attacks.

The whole universe is ready when you are. So claim and accept the rich abundance God has for you now!

Prosperity Prayer: Letting go of lack, I claim abundance, and I accept it now!

PRO$PER NOW! #83

TEN WAYS to expand your
prosperity mental equivalent:

1. Mentally accept more than you now have.
2. Visualize more money flowing into your
   hands.
3. Develop unlimited ideas of prosperity.
4. Eliminate all limiting, poverty thoughts.
5. Think "plenty" instead of 'not enough.'
6. Feel rich inside.
7. Praise the power within you and feel it
   expand.
8. Believe and act as if you already have your
   new high level income.
9. Establish harmony in your world.
10. Believe in and live by the spiritual law,
    "God is the Source of my supply."

Prosperity Prayer: Divinely guided, I
expand my prosperity mental equivalent and
I richly prosper now.

HOW TO create your prosperity mental equivalent:

1. Get clearly in mind, the object of your desire.
2. Use Prosperity Prayers, such as are included in this book, to strengthen your conviction and confidence.
3. Daily pray the Prosperity Prayers audibly as part of your daily meditation times.
4. Totally identify with your desire. Feel your oneness with it. Act as though it is already so.
5. Keep quiet. Do not talk to just anyone about what you want to achieve. Secrecy and deep faith have great prospering power.

Prosperity Prayer: **Divinely guided, I am creating a new prosperity mental equivalent. I easily prosper now!**

PRO$PER NOW! #85

YOUR prosperity is deeply rooted in what you are, personally. You must build a mental equivalent in which you accept yourself as a prosperous person. Here are some attitudes of mind and behavior patterns to help you create a true and productive prosperity mental equivalent:

Vision. Integrity. Ambition. Conviction. Loyalty. Persistence. Responsibility. Sincerity. Tolerance. Thrift. Self-confidence Willpower. Tithing. Loving kindness. Peace. Sharing. Gratitude. Knowing God as the source of your prosperity. Regular times of prayer and meditation.

Add to these the practice of the presence of God in all that you think, feel, say, and do. God is love and the fulfillment of your desires.

Prosperity Prayer: Divinely guided, I think, feel, speak, and act prosperously.

PRO$PER NOW! #86

CHARLES FILLMORE wrote, "In the great Mind of God there is no thought of lack, and such a thought has no rightful place in your mind. It is your birthright to be prosperous, regardless of who you are or where you may be. Cultivate the habit of thinking about abundance everywhere present, not only in the forms of imagination but in physical visible forms." (*Prosperity* - Unity House)

Imagination is wonderfully creative and you should use yours to see, within, the riches of God and to accept them as yours. But it is equally important for you to see them manifesting in your life in practical, usable form.

Decide to be supremely prosperous inwardly and outwardly in every wonderful way.

Prosperity Prayer: I am grateful that I am inwardly and outwardly wonderfully prospered now.

THERE is no situation that cannot be corrected, no trouble so difficult that there cannot be found a satisfying solution to. It may take time, but it can be found. Regardless of your condition--poor health, poor finances, unhappiness--you *can* rise into healthy, happy, prosperous living.

You can when you dare to act. Even if you enjoy a wonderful level of prosperity, you can move on to higher levels. There are no limits to the riches of God, except for those limits you place upon yourself. (From the author's book, *How I CAN Have Everything!*)

Your prosperity is unlimited because God is unlimited, and God is your ever-present resource. You need only to back up your faith with action. It is really up to you. You can be prosperous--very prosperous--and you should be!

Prosperity Prayer: I can be prosperous and I back up my belief with faith and *action*.

PRO$PER NOW! #88

LOVE is great prospering power especially when it is expressed in forgiveness. Holding on to anger severely blocks your prosperity. It is wise to forgive quickly and completely, allowing nothing of a hurtful nature to remain in your consciousness.

The Buddhist says. "If a man foolishly does me wrong, I will return to him the protection of my ungrudging love. The more evil comes from him, the more good shall go from me." The Hindu says, "Return good for evil, overcome anger by love; hatred never ceases by hatred, but by love."

By taking a positive, loving attitude, you quickly make peace concerning whatever comes and the way is open and clear for you to prosper.

Prosperity Prayer: I quickly and completely forgive everyone and everything. I send love to all. I am free and I prosper now!

PRO$PER NOW! #89

FEAR of losing your money can be great, and destructive, even among the wealthy. A wealthy businessman literally worried himself sick, although to all appearances, he had nothing to fear. Yet, he had a tremendous fear of losing his money. Because the prosperity law of tithing gives the one who faithfully tithes, divine protection, he does not fear losing his money. When this man learned this, and began to tithe, he stopped fearing and became healthy.

By the act of tithing men make God their partner in their financial transactions.

When you believe that you are helping to keep God's work going on earth, you cannot help but know that God is actively helping you to prosper. You know, there is nothing to fear.

Prosperity Prayer: As a tither, I know there is nothing to fear. God is my source, and I am always abundantly prospered.

DO YOU love happy financial surprises? Most people do. They are much better than the other kind! Happy financial surprises is the premise of my book, *How To Have 'Unexpected' Income.* In this book is a very powerful Prayer-Treatment for 'Unexpected' Income. This has been used by thousands of people to attract to them, a great variety of happy financial, and other wonderful, surprises.

One person was given, out-of-the-blue, $50,000! Now, *that* is happy! It doesn't happen to everyone, but numerous people have used the Prayer-Treatment and have reaped a great harvest of 'unexpected' income. That is because they opened their minds to the vast abundance of God, and unlimited the channels by which to be more abundantly prospered.

Prosperity Prayer: I love happy financial surprises. They are coming to me now through God's unlimited channels.

PRO$PER NOW! #91

DO YOU consciously or unconsciously limit your financial supply? Many people do. In so doing, they believe that not many doors, or channels, of financial supply are open to them. Actually, the opposite is true. The channels of God's supply are infinite. Accept that all financial doors are open, all financial channels are free.

You will find it very beneficial to more greatly expand your realization of the boundlessness of God's riches for you. You might even attract millions to you more easily than you may think. Using the *Pro$per Now* Prosperity Prayers, speaking them over and over, will help, but especially the one for today.

Prosperity Prayer: All financial doors are open, all financial channels are free, and the millions that are mine by divine right, now come to me in God's own wonderful way!

95

LIFE IS CHOICE*. It is one choice after another, which is to say that it is always decision time. Years ago, I discovered that I hated to make decisions. I would do everything I could to avoid doing so. Often I would depend on other people to make decision for me because, as I eventually learned, I didn't trust myself, and was unaware that God had given me the wisdom to make right decisions. Fortunately, I made a very important decision: *Change my thinking.*

Thankfully, you have the freedom to choose. You may choose whatever you want: To be sad or happy, sick or well, angry or loving, poor or prosperous. Each morning take a few minutes before getting out of bed to make your choices for the day. Making positive choices, pays rich dividends.

Prosperity Prayer: Today I choose life love, joy, health, peace, and prosperity!

*Life is Choice, a new book by the author. (Pub. - late 2003.)

PRO$PER NOW! #93

ARE your limitations working for you? While attending a workshop facilitated by Harry Morgan Moses, founder of Creative Enhancement, Inc. and the New Thought Center (www.newthought.com), in San Diego, he said to stop arguing for your limitations. He also said that we should be aware that they are not working for us.

How about you? What limitations have you placed on yourself and your prosperity? If you have created a belief system that does not serve you well, it is time for a divine adjustment. With God's help, boldly let go of old limiting beliefs and acquire new prospering ones. Accept, right now, that you do live in the midst of God's unlimited bounty and that all of God's good is yours. Claim and accept your share.

Prosperity Prayer: **Right now, I live in the midst of God's bounty. I thankfully claim and accept my share, and I prosper now!**

BLESSING PAYS. When a colleague would go into a restaurant, he would ask the waiters if they would like to increase their tips by at least 50%. If they said yes, he told them to silently and sincerely bless the people at each table they served. Some thought him a little weird, but others did as he suggested. He said he received numerous letters from them attesting to the power of blessing the people at the tables they served, and their increased tips.

Blessing carries a powerful vibration because it is a highly energized spiritual activity. It is nothing less than love moving from heart to heart. Try lovingly blessing people you work with, your money, and everything and everybody, and see what happens. I believe you will be pleasantly surprised.

Prosperity Prayer: I lovingly bless everything and everybody in my world.

PRO$PER NOW! #95

WHEN your financial supply seems blocked, check up on your giving. There is great energy in generosity in that it radiates magnetic power. It causes all manner of good to be drawn to you such as ideas, helpful people, prospering opportunities, and the prospering substance of God.

Prosperity is not just about receiving, but even more about giving - being generous with your money, talents, and love. If you were to draw water from a well, using an old-fashioned pump, you'd have to prime the pump first. The Universe is in balance. Your part is to keep the flow of divine substance moving by generously passing it on to others. Thus as you richly bless others, you are blessed.

Prosperity Prayer: I am a free and open channel through which God blesses everyone, and we all abundantly prosper now.

THE WAY is always open. When, in your quest to prosper, the way seems to be blocked, it is good to remember that God always opens a way. In the movie, *The Sound Of Music,* when a door was apparently closed, Maria realized that God always opens a window.

There is an old Unity prayer (see below) which I have prayed numerous times, and the way always opens not only prosperity doors, but windows, too.

This is an excellent way to "golden key" a difficult financial situation, and it *always* works because you remember, God is your source, and that your supply is always at hand waiting for your acceptance of it.

Prosperity Prayer: God is my instant, constant, and abundant source of supply, for which I give thanks. God opens ways where to human sense there appears to be no way.

"PROSPERITY is a way of living and thinking, not just the possession of money. Poverty is a way of living and thinking, not just the lack of money. Fear of economic insecurity evaporates as we move into an awareness of abundance." - Mary Mannin Morrissey, *Building Your Field of Dreams.*

Usually, when people have plenty of money, they are thought of as being prosperous. However, it is not money alone that makes them that way. It is their consciousness of abundance, which is a true connection with all of God's wealth within, that out-pictures in money and other things making life more enjoyable and productive. When you have this, you have no fear of financial insecurity.

Prosperity Prayer: I think and live in the consciousness of God's abundance. I am safe and secure, and truly prospered.

PRO$PER NOW! #98

A BUSINESSMAN in Mississippi wrote the following to me: "I want to thank you for the lessons you teach through your writings which I try to reinforce everyday regarding my prosperity; writing my goals, expectations, thanksgiving, and tithing. I am grateful that I now have three pieces of income property, and am about to close on #4. These acquisitions are big steps toward my ultimate goal of creating large commercial, high-quality income-producing properties. Thank you for your help."

This is further evidence of the power of writing down your goals, and having the qualities this man wrote about in his letter. He is creating his prosperity mentally, first, and it is working for him. It will work you☐ too!

Prosperity Prayer: I create my prosperity mentally first, and I prosper now!

PRO$PER NOW! #99

SOMETIMES you may feel discouraged, especially if a goal is not realized on time, or something happens to cause your financial supply to diminish. But when that happens do whatever you can to raise your vibrations. Do not waste time in feeling sorry for yourself because that sends the wrong message to the Universe.

Do not waste time or energy in talking about how bad things seem to be. That, too, sends the wrong message to the Universe. The Universe is wholly willing to give you whatever you focus the great energy of your thinking upon, so be sure you send the right message by thinking upwardly, positively, and prosperously. Using these daily inspirations and Prosperity Prayers will help you raise your vibrations to a higher level and help you stay there.

Prosperity Prayer: Thinking upwardly, positively and prosperously, the Universe prospers me now!

PRO$PER NOW! #100

DR. ERNEST HOLMES said: "It is a great mistake to say, *'Take what you wish, for you can have anything you like.'* We do not take what we *wish*, but we do attract to ourselves that which is like our thought. Man must become more if he desires to draw greater good into his life."

In reality, everything is yours, but it is only as true as you make it. Wishing doesn't make it so. You always attract the correspondent of what you are in consciousness. Step by step, thought by thought, you create within yourself, the prosperity consciousness that is out-pictured in your life as prosperous living. *Be* that which you desire to *have* and you *will* have it. Thus, you prosper now, and every day, as it is your divine right to do.

Prosperity Prayer: It is true - I am prosperity. Every day, in every way, I prosper now!

PRO$PER NOW! #101

ARE you abnormal? Wallace D. Wattles wrote in, *The Science of Getting Rich,* "There is nothing wrong with the desire to get rich. The desire for riches is really the desire for a richer, fuller, and more abundant life; and that desire is praiseworthy. The man who does not desire to live more abundantly is abnormal, and so the man who does not desire to have money enough to buy all he wants is abnormal."

If you were abnormal, you wouldn't be reading the inspirations and praying the Prosperity Prayers on the pages of this book. There would be no point in daily investing the small amount of time, energy, and discipline requiresd for you to fulfill your desire to create a more prosperous life. It is normal and supremely right for you to be rich.

Prosperity Prayer: Yea! It's supremely right for me to be rich! And I am!

PRO$PER NOW! #106

TRUST the process. Here are four rules by which to demonstrate all the prosperity you could ever desire. 1. Ask. 2. Believe. 3. Let go and let it happen. 4. Be thankful.

1. **Ask** God for whatever you want in the realization that with God all thing are possible.

2. **Believe** in trusting faith that good is manifesting for you in God's own good way, and it is doing so now.

3. **Let go and let it happen.** It is God that brings it forth, not you. Relax and trust the process.

4. **Be thankful.** Give thanks just as though you have already received what you have asked for. Thanksgiving opens and keeps open the avenues of abundant supply.

Prosperity Prayer: **I ask, believe, let go, and give thanks for my rich, abundant supply, and I prosper now.**

PRO$PER NOW! #107

ITIS never too late for you to prosper, unless you accept that it is. Many people have been prospered after the age of sixty. Colonel Sanders, of Kentucky Fried Chicken fame, is one example. After working for other people until about sixty, he came up with a better idea, and created the KFC stores. He made millions in the process.

Some people who have been laid off because of company downsizing, have gone into business for themselves. This often results in creating fortunes, but it didn't happen until they left the old limited life and opened their minds to making it on their own, with God's help, of course. No matter your age or circumstances, it is never too late to prosper.

Prosperity Prayer: It is never too late. Divinely guided, I am easily moving into my greater prosperity now.

PRO$PER NOW! #108

WHAT are you in stride with? Are you in stride with a downward spiral of life, or with the upward spiral of life? Upward, onward, and forward is the natural impulse of the Universe. It is unnatural, therefore, for you to experience less and less. If you do, it simply means that you have gotten out of stride with the upward, progressive movement of life.

A businesswoman realized she needed help and sought out a spiritual counselor who helped her get back in harmony with the upward, progressive flow of life. The result: This businesswoman became more prosperous than ever!

There is a mighty stream of prosperity for you. Step into and go with the flow!

Prosperity Prayer: I am in stride with the upward, progressive movement of life.

PRO$PER NOW! #109

PROSPERITY does not come to you by trying to manipulate people and events. Neither is your prosperity subject to human limitations or fluctuations. Prosperity is a spiritual idea, therefore, it is a constant. The goodness of life is all about you now. It is an alive, moving, powerful force. Open yourself to it. Rejoice, because everything you need to fulfill your prosperity goals is at hand. It is yours now.

Accept that it is your divine right to have whatever you want. It is the divine impulse in you seeking expression. Do not stop it up. Let it flow! Let this universal creative energy move through your mind, your body, and your actions. Now is the time. No longer delay it. Let it prosper you now!

Prosperity Prayer: No more obstacles, no more delays. I now experience prospering days!

PRO$PER NOW! #110

TEN things to remember about demonstrating prosperity:

1. The mental process necessary to a greater income is a matter of recognition, acceptance, and belief. This mental experience must precede any material manifestation.

2. Supply is fundamentally an invisible thing; it is receiving into your consciousness the Spirit of god, which created all things from the beginning of which all things are formed.

3. The metaphysical method of demonstrating prosperity is to put the prospering ideas to work.

4. Poverty is a state of mind. We bring about this manifestation by our negative recognition, acceptance, and belief.

5. We overcome poverty by mastering the sense of every kind of lack. *(Continued on next page)*

Prosperity Prayer: I recognize, accept, and believe, God in me is the source of my supply, and He prospers me now!

TEN things to remember about demonstrating prosperity: *(Continued)*

6. We look not to the world for things, persons, and places in solving our problem of supply but look within our own consciousness.

7. We master the sense of want by building an inner sense of plenty.

8. We can have anything we desire if we believe that we already have it.

9. Prosperity is not a matter of education, training, working, saving, investing, struggling, or denying yourself. It is a matter of getting into harmony with the Law of your own individual consciousness and then following that Law to it logical conclusion.

10. The permanent source of our prosperity lies in our power to possess and to mold in our thought, the Universal God Substance.

Prosperity Prayer: **My abundance consciousness mightily prospers me now.**

PRO$PER NOW! #112

"BEHOLD THE TURTLE! -- It makes progress only when it sticks its neck out!" This caption was on a poster, with a big green turtle, which I used to have. When I would look at the poster, I would think," I must be making progress because I stick my neck out so much." When a turtle sticks its neck out, it means that it's moving forward. To move forward means that you must be willing to risk everything.

Your desire to prosper requires you to take risks, to let go of the familiar, even things you thought were all important, but they must go, too. Making progress in your quest to prosper requires you to be bold in your decisions and actions so your new, more prosperous life may be enjoyed. So, dare to prosper! Stick your neck out. Don't look back. Boldly move forward into your new prosperity!

Prosperity Prayer: Divinely guided, I boldly move forward. I dare to prosper now!

PRO$PER NOW! #113

ONE time I when I waxed my car, I wasn't satisfied with the finish because it didn't really shine. So I purchased a bottle of cleaner, more wax, and attacked the car again. Not only did the old wax and oxidation come off, but an amazing amount of dirt and grime as well! Then I applied the new wax and you can just imagine how brilliantly the car shone when I finished!

It seems that too often we tend to apply something over what already is without removing the old stuff first. If you want your prosperity to "shine," and I am sure you do, then some deep cleaning may be in order. This means to dig into your consciousness and get rid of old programming: lack-concepts, and beliefs in limitation so that there is a solid basis for your new, shiny prosperity.

Prosperity Prayer: Letting go the old, I easily move into my new, shiny prosperity.

PRO$PER NOW! #114

OUR loving Father-God did not create a Universe of deprivation but one of grand abundance. But He left it up to each individual to claim and accept what each would have. He gave to each of us the tools of mind and the substance needed for producing prosperity in our lives.

It is up to you to do with what you have. Make no excuse. Do not waste a moment in thinking any other way or about anything which is not prosperity-producing. Make room in your consciousness for rich, beautiful, healthy, happy thoughts, ideas, and attitudes, and your life will be beautiful and bountiful. It is God's intention for you to enjoy more and more of His riches. You have been authorized to do so. So, do it!

Prosperity Prayer: I now enjoy my new, beautiful and bountiful, happy, prosperous life!

PRO$PER NOW! #115

TRUE prosperity means not only having plenty of money, but being rich in friends. What good is plenty of money if you don't have the love and companionship of people who love you for who and what you are rather than how much money you have? This is not to say that having plenty of money is not important. But friendships are equally so.

A person I know, who has millions is poor in true friends, while another person has plenty of money, and friends. The latter is understandably happier, and wealthier. On the other hand, you can be prosperous in friendships, but poor financially. Do not make the mistake that this is okay. It is healthy be wealthy in *every* area of life.

Prosperity Prayer: I give thanks that I am prosperous in money and friends.

PRO$PER NOW! #116

IT IS interesting that many people who are considered to be very successful in the business world, experience poor health. They give much time and energy to gaining financial success, but neglect their bodies in the process. Some people mistakenly believe they can put just about anything into their bodies, and give little thought to the care of them.

If you are unable to enjoy your wealth because of ill-health, that is a misfortune. What good does it do if you have to spend a large amount of your wealth on trying to get your body well again? Being prosperous in health is just as important as in finances. It's a vital and healthy part of the overall prosperity picture. Being the picture of health means all areas of life.

Prosperity Prayer: I prosper now in health, friends, and money.

A FELLOW who was financially wealthy, wasn't happy. He gave more of his attention to creating a very successful financial life for himself. He could "drive a hard bargain," and had a knack for being in the right place at the right time when it came to increasing his financial fortune. But he did so at the expense of true happiness.

Fortunately, he sought help admitting that he wasn't truly happy. He wanted to know what he could do without sacrificing his financial wealth. He was advised to go within and commune with God, the source of true happiness. He was then told to relax and have fun and to no longer be so serious about creating his financial fortune. Doing as advised resulted in great happiness and improved financial success. And, he had lots of fun in the process!

Prosperity Prayer: I relax and let God, the source of health, wealth, and happiness have more fun as me!

"NEEDS are not the real issue. When we focus upon what we lack, we experience anxiety and a sense of inadequacy. The new millennium demands that we put aside our needs. A life of quality does not begin with what seems to be lacking. It begins as we turn attention to what is present." - - Jim Rosemergy - *Even Mystics Have Bills To Pay*

We all have needs, but giving energy to needs, never fulfills them. It is only when we rise above needs into the conscious presence of God, that we are fulfilled. Even God cannot provide for us if our attention is on our needs because we are focusing on what we lack instead of what we have. Our consciousness of God is our true prosperity. Knowing this, we are richly and abundantly prospered.

Prosperity Prayer: **My consciousness of God, as my source, is my true prosperity.**

HARMONY is essential for true success and prosperity. Napoleon Hill, author of *Think And Grow Rich*, said that the most important thing great industrialists had, in their Master Mind groups, was harmony. He said that without harmony, nothing worthwhile could be accomplished. Harmony is the main ingredient in any quest, especially, the quest for true success.

In a Master Mind group, and in every area of life, harmony is essential because this leads to agreement. "Where two or more agree on a thing, it will come to pass." Harmony is a divine law, which your growing prosperity requires for you to be successful. This includes your home, work, play, everything.

Prosperity Prayer: I am in harmony with my world and the natural flow of prosperity. I prosper now!

CELEBRATE PROSPERITY! Every day, make your growing prosperity a reason for celebration. My good friend, Larry James, says to, "Celebrate Love." He means to celebrate the activity of love and all that love is. The same applies to prosperity. Celebrate the divine activity of the substance of God as it flows more freely and abundantly in your life!

Celebrate means to praise, observe, and magnify. Praise your growing prosperity. Observe with joy and gratitude how it is multiplying and magnifying because you are playing by the rules. You are remembering that God is your source and your prosperity, and that money is God in action to be used for good. Celebrate your prosperity as divinely sanctioned. How good it is to prosper now! So, Celebrate! Enjoy! Praise and give thanks! This is only the beginning!

Prosperity Prayer: I celebrate my ever-growing prosperity!

SOME of the prospering messages in this book are excepts from the author's other books, and can also be found on the Pro$per Now page on his website: www.GoldenKeyMinistry.com.

Remember, in your quest for prosperity, to Live Life Lovingly is essential, and that love is the most important thing of all. The more love you put into your prosperity quest, and all that you undertake, the happier, healthier, more fulfilled you are and the more real is your prosperity.

You will find it helpful to not only pray the Prosperity Prayers audibly, but to take them into the Silence and meditate on them. Your true prosperity is within you, first.

I trust this book inspires you to more easily travel the prosperity road, to stay on course, and to enjoy the rich abundance God has for you.. Have a wonderful journey and enjoy the trip!

I am always happy to hear from my readers and to learn how my books help them. Please write to me.

John Wolcott Adams
P O Box 30989, Phoenix, AZ 85046 USA

Enjoy all of John Wolcott Adams' inspiring books:

Positively Alive!
How To Have 'Unexpected' Income
Power Words For Prosperous Living
How I CAN Have Everything!
Thirty Days To A Better Life
BE What You Are: LOVE
Pro$per Now!
Life Is Choice

Buy these books where you purchased this one. To order directly from the author, please use the order form on page 127.

Give copies of these books to your friends.

PRO$PER NOW! Inspirations and Prosperity Prayers are on the author's website:
www.GoldenKeyMinistry.com

To contact the author, send an e-mail to:
RevJohn@GoldenKeyMinistry.com
(Please mention the title of this book.)

Order all of the author's books.

___Pro$per Now!	$14.95
___Be What You Are: LOVE	$8.95
___How To Have 'Unexpected' Income	$8.95
___Positively Alive!	$10.95
___Thirty Days To A Better Life	$5.95
___Power Words For Prosperous Living	$8.95
___How I CAN Have Everything!	$12.95
___Life Is Choice *(late 2003)*	$14.95

Order 10 or more copes of any of these titles (mix or match) and deduct 20% from your order. Prices in US dollars & include postage except Canada, Mexico & Overseas, please add 40% to total cost.

Send your order to: John Wolcott Adams
P. O. Box 30989, Phoenix AZ 85046-0989 USA
Credit Card orders: www.GoldenKeyMinistry.com

Name_____

Address_____

City, State, ZIP _____

Total amount enclosed for books: $_____

Contribution to Golden Key Ministry: $_____

(You may photocopy this page.)

PRO$PER NOW!

Why wait?

Open your mind and heart now to the creative spirit of God that forever moves in and through you, and keep them open. Let His creative spirit bless and multiply all that you are, have, give, and receive. As you do, all of God's rich abundance--that is your natural heritage--becomes a permanent part of your consciousness, and your life.

- - John Wolcott Adams,
"Positively Alive"

128

www.ingramcontent.com/pod-product-compliance
Lightning Source LLC
Chambersburg PA
CBHW020208200326
41521CB00005BA/299